I0796269

Olivia Rodrigo
Jackie Golusky
childsworld.com

Published by The Child's World®
800-599-READ • www.childsworld.com

Photography Credits
Photographs ©: Joel C. Ryan/Invision/AP Images, cover, 1; Sthanlee B. Mirador/Sipa USA/Alamy Live News/Alamy, 5; Flickr, 6; Kathy Hutchins/Shutterstock Images, 9, 13, 18, 24; Ken Wolter/Shutterstock Images, 10; Katharine Hale/Red Line Editorial, 11; Chris Pizzello/Invision/AP Images, 14; Jasen Wright/Shutterstock Images, 17; Shutterstock Images, 21; Paul R. Giunta/Invision/AP Images, 23; Lawrence Jackson/Biden White House, 27; Kevin Mazur/Getty Images for FireAid/Getty Images Entertainment/Getty Images, 28; Design elements from Shutterstock Images

ISBN Information
9781503875746 (Reinforced Library Binding)
9781503876699 (Portable Document Format)
9781503877191 (Online Multi-user eBook)
9781503877818 (Electronic Publication)

LCCN 2025938200

Printed in the United States of America

ABOUT THE AUTHOR

Jackie Golusky is a writer who lives near the Twin Cities in Minnesota. She graduated from Hamline University with a degree in creative writing. Her cat, Remmy, is her writing companion.

TABLE of CONTENTS

CHAPTER ONE

Iconic Artist

On February 4, 2024, Olivia Rodrigo stepped onto the stage. A piano played as Rodrigo began to sing "vampire" at the 2024 Grammy Awards. This is the music industry's biggest award show. Rodrigo belted out the top tune of her second album, titled *GUTS*. Some people in the audience joined in. Music megastar Taylor Swift sang and danced along. Rodrigo's "vampire" was her third song to reach number one on the *Billboard* Hot 100. This chart lists the most popular songs in the United States. It includes all types of music.

Olivia Rodrigo arrived on the red carpet at the 2024 Grammy Awards wearing a white dress.

It was not Rodrigo's first time at the Grammy Awards. Her first album, *SOUR*, won Best Pop Vocal Album in 2022. Her hit song "drivers license" won Best Pop Solo Performance. And Rodrigo was named Best New Artist.

Throughout the *GUTS* World Tour, Rodrigo played instruments such as the piano and guitar.

In 2024, Rodrigo had returned to the Grammy Awards with an **acclaimed** record. Fans loved her music. As the last notes of "vampire" rang out, the audience stood and applauded. A few weeks later, on February 23, 2024, Rodrigo kicked off her *GUTS* World Tour. It was a major year for the musician.

Rodrigo had come a long way. She was always interested in performing and writing songs. She had begun as a young actor. She performed in local talent shows and school plays. When she tried out for different roles, she was told no again and again. But Rodrigo pushed forward. She landed lead roles in Disney Channel's *Bizaardvark* and *High School Musical: The Musical: The Series (HSM:TM:TS)*. But the release of "drivers license" shot her to stardom. And with two hit albums at a young age, she continued to amaze fans around the world.

CHAPTER TWO

Start as an Actor

Olivia Isabel Rodrigo was born on February 20, 2003, in Murrieta, California. She grew up an only child. She is Filipino American. Olivia's father, Chris, is of Filipino descent. He worked as a **therapist**. Olivia's mother, Jennifer, has German and Irish **heritage**. She worked as an elementary teacher.

Growing up in Temecula, California, Olivia was very close with her parents. They shared their love of music with Olivia. They signed her up for singing lessons when she was just 5 years old. Olivia's voice teacher was Jennifer Dustman. Dustman worked with many young musicians and child actors. She was impressed with the young singer's voice. Dustman knew Olivia needed to be on a stage to share her talent. Olivia loved to perform on stage, too. So Dustman helped Olivia practice for talent shows and contests.

When Olivia's grandfather held her as a baby, he said she would be a performing artist.

At the same time, Dustman also noticed how expressive Olivia was when she sang. She encouraged Olivia's parents to sign her up for acting classes.

It would help grow her talents. Olivia performed in school plays. She also **auditioned** for roles in movies and TV commercials. Olivia's parents drove her 90 miles (145 km) to Los Angeles, California, for auditions. Though Olivia did not land many of the roles, she did not stop trying.

At about 9 years old, Olivia's parents signed her up for piano lessons. At first, she hated playing the piano. The lessons were hard. She often cried before them. But about a year later, Olivia grew to love the piano. The piano helped her come up with songs. She sang lyrics she had written to simple melodies.

In 2011, Olivia sang "Don't Rain on My Parade" by Barbra Streisand at her town's Boys & Girls Clubs singing competition.

***Grace Stirs Up Success* is a movie based on the Grace American Girl doll and books.**

Finally, Olivia's auditioning paid off. At 10 years old, Olivia landed the lead role in the American Girl movie *Grace Stirs Up Success*. Olivia starred as Grace. The movie released in 2015.

In 2016, Olivia landed a new role with Disney. The show was called *Bizaardvark*. Olivia had to make a choice between school and acting. She would need to move to Los Angeles to be closer to the job. She would also need to leave public school and be homeschooled. Together Olivia and her parents made the decision to move. It was a difficult choice. But it was also Olivia's dream to perform.

On *Bizaardvark*, Olivia met Madison Hu. Madison was her costar. The two played best friends on the show. Olivia and Madison quickly became friends offscreen, too. They called each other soulmates. After *Bizaardvark* ended in 2019, Olivia did not know what to do. She had just turned 14 years old. She struggled to know who she was. Adults kept asking her what she wanted to do, and she did not know how to answer them. But soon Olivia figured out her next move.

Olivia took on a new role in 2019. She starred in *HSM:TM:TS*. The Disney show followed a group of students at East High. Olivia played Nini Salazar-Roberts. Olivia moved to Salt Lake City, Utah, for the job.

Olivia (left) played Paige Olvera and Madison Hu (right) played Frankie Wong in *Bizaardvark*. The characters sang and made music videos.

Olivia wrote a song for *HSM:TM:TS* with costar Joshua Bassett. It was called "Just for a Moment."

While Olivia was acting, she still wrote and sang songs. She posted a song on Instagram, and it received many likes. The show's **producers** showed Olivia's song to the music team. The music team liked her songwriting. They asked her to write a song for Nini to perform. Olivia was excited.

In the fourth episode of *HSM:TM:TS*, Olivia wrote and sang "All I Want." The song expressed Nini's emotions after a breakup. "All I Want" was a hit for the show. It also rose to the *Billboard* Hot 100 chart. While Olivia was making a name for herself as an actor, she was also gaining popularity as a singer-songwriter. The song's success was only the beginning of her music journey.

WRITER'S BLOCK

In the second season of *HSM:TM:TS*, Olivia wrote another song. It was called "The Rose Song." It followed Nini as she struggled with writer's block. Writer's block is when someone is writing and cannot figure out what to say. Olivia has experienced writer's block, too.

CHAPTER THREE

SOUR Megastar

After making music for *HSM:TM:TS,* Olivia began writing songs that expressed more of her feelings. In 2020, she signed with a record label. A record label is a company that helps record and sell a musician's work.

In January 2021, Olivia released her first single. In music, a single is a song that is released on its own. It may be the first song from an upcoming album. Olivia's hit single "drivers license" showcased her voice. It also **demonstrated** her songwriting skills.

A recording studio is a space that musicians may use to record vocals and instruments. It has tools such as microphones and other sound equipment.

The song "drivers license" was number one on the *Billboard* Hot 100 for 8 weeks. At 17 years old, Olivia was the youngest person to ever lead the chart. The hit song also set new records for the most-streamed song on Spotify, an audio streaming site. It reached about 17 million streams in a day.

Olivia attended the Music Hitmakers Brunch in 2021. When "drivers license" released on Spotify that year, it became the most-streamed non-holiday song in a week with about 66 million streams.

Olivia had planned to release an extended play (EP). An EP usually has six songs or fewer. But after the success of "drivers license," she knew she wanted to write even more songs. A full album would showcase her singing and songwriting skills. Olivia worked every day for about 13 hours. She helped write every song on the album. She worked with her producer Dan Nigro. Together, they came up with the album name *SOUR*.

In April 2021, Olivia released her second hit single, "deja vu." The song reached number eight on the *Billboard* Hot 100. Olivia's last single for the album was "good 4 u." It also led the *Billboard* Hot 100. It made *SOUR* the first album to have three singles enter the chart's top ten. On May 21, 2021, Olivia released her **debut** album, *SOUR,* to the world. Olivia quickly became a worldwide sensation.

In 2022, Olivia attended her first-ever Grammy Awards. She was nominated for seven awards. At the show, she won Best Pop Solo Performance, Best New Artist, and Best Pop Vocal Album. She gave a short speech after accepting her awards. Olivia shared her excitement about winning her first Grammy Award. She thanked her parents for their support. Olivia also looked forward to creating more music for her fans.

CREDITING ARTISTS

Olivia has often said she admires Taylor Swift. But some people pointed out similarities between their songs. With many people speaking out about potential plagiarism, Olivia eventually credited Swift for "1 step forward, 3 steps back" and "deja vu." Plagiarism is when someone takes another person's work and says it is their own. Olivia also credited two songwriters in the band Paramore on her song "good 4 u." By giving these musicians credits, they received some of the money made from the songs.

RODRIGO'S TOP MUSIC AWARDS

As a growing artist, Olivia Rodrigo has claimed many awards for her singing and songwriting skills. Here are a few of the top awards she and her works have earned throughout her career.

3 GRAMMY AWARDS

2022

- Best Pop Vocal Album (*SOUR*)
- Best Pop Solo Performance ("drivers license")
- Best New Artist (*SOUR*)

7 *BILLBOARD* MUSIC AWARDS

2022

- Top New Artist
- Top Female Artist
- Top Hot 100 Artist
- Top Streaming Songs Artist
- Top Radio Songs Artist
- Top *Billboard* Global 200 Artist
- Top *Billboard* 200 Album (*SOUR*)

4 MTV VIDEO MUSIC AWARDS

2021

- Song of the Year ("drivers license")
- Best New Artist
- PUSH Performance of the Year ("drivers license")

2023

- Best Editing ("vampire")

4 iHEARTRADIO MUSIC AWARDS

2022

- Female Artist of the Year
- Best New Pop Artist
- TikTok Bop of the Year ("good 4 u")

2024

- Pop Album of the Year (*GUTS*)

CHAPTER FOUR

Spilling Her *GUTS*

With the success of *SOUR*, Rodrigo was excited to announce her first tour. She was going to perform her songs live in concerts. She spent many days practicing her songs. She exercised to keep her stamina strong. It was hard work singing and moving across a large stage. On April 2, 2022, Rodrigo kicked off the *SOUR* tour in San Francisco, California. She traveled across parts of the United States and Europe.

Many fans were eager to hear Rodrigo's songs live. Tickets to her *SOUR* tour sold out in minutes.

At the end of the *SOUR* tour, Rodrigo felt a lot of pressure. She loved to write songs, but she was worried about what people would think of her new songs. But Rodrigo knew she had to focus on making songs she enjoyed the most. She wrote songs that she would want to hear on the radio. She did not try to top the success of her earlier songs or please anyone.

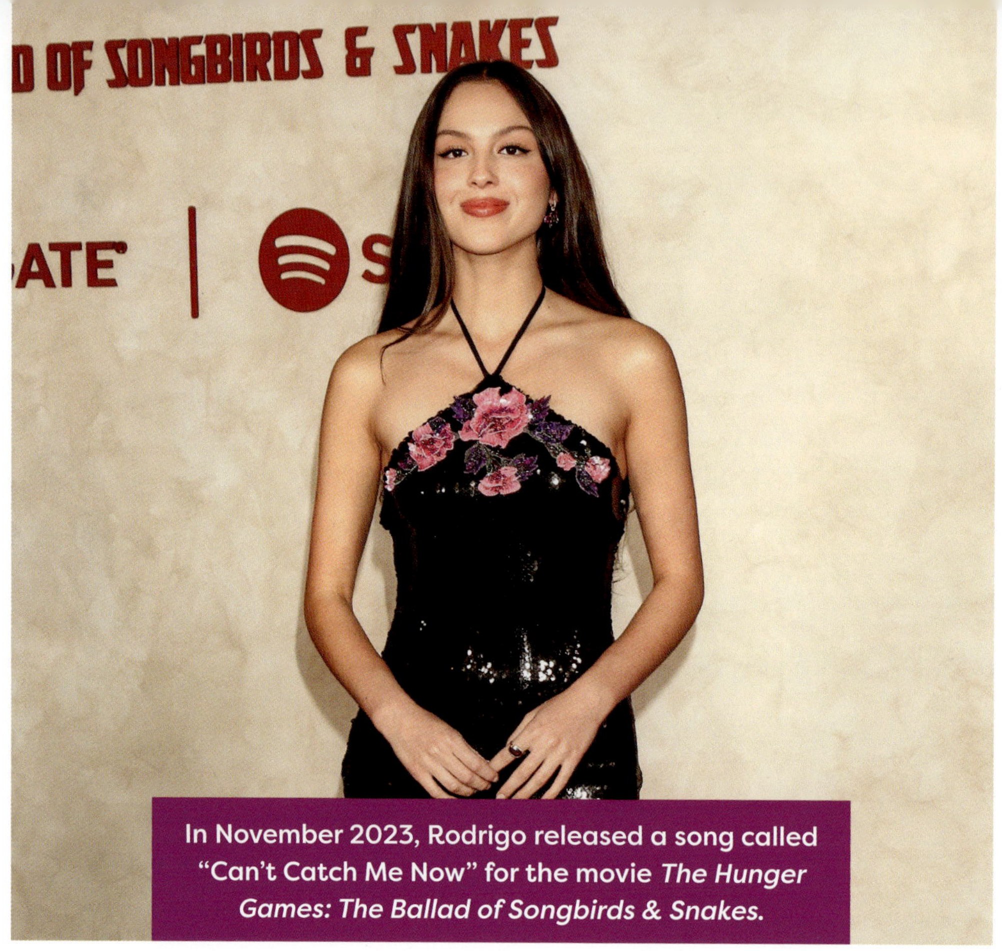

In November 2023, Rodrigo released a song called "Can't Catch Me Now" for the movie *The Hunger Games: The Ballad of Songbirds & Snakes.*

In June 2023, Rodrigo released the first single off her second album. The song was called "vampire." Fans loved it. The song soared to number one on the *Billboard* Hot 100. Rodrigo became the first artist to have lead singles off her first two albums hit number one.

In September 2023, Rodrigo's second album, *GUTS,* was released. The songs showcased Rodrigo's growing talent as an artist. All 12 songs hit the *Billboard* Hot 100's top 40 songs. Rodrigo's *GUTS* sold even more albums than *SOUR.*

After the release of *GUTS*, Rodrigo was busy preparing for her first world tour. It spanned places in North America, South America, Europe, and Asia. The first night was on February 23, 2024. Rodrigo performed with her band. She sang and danced with backup dancers. She also played slower piano **ballads**. She even flew on a moon around the stadium. This let her be closer to the crowd. At the end, confetti stars fell onto fans.

In March 2024, Rodrigo released the **deluxe** version of *GUTS*. The album included five additional songs. This version was called *GUTS: spilled*. Rodrigo had already been performing "obsessed" from her deluxe album on the *GUTS* World Tour. Fans were now excited to have it on streaming services. On March 22, fans voted online that Rodrigo's album was the best release that week.

CHAPPELL ROAN

Singer Chappell Roan was one of the opening acts for Rodrigo's *GUTS* World Tour. The two singers shared the same music producer, Dan Nigro. Roan also helped sing backup vocals on both of Rodrigo's albums. Together, the singers performed Roan's popular song "HOT TO GO!" for Rodrigo's Netflix concert special.

Rodrigo has often used her voice to stand up for causes she cares about, too. In 2021, she visited the White House to encourage young people to get vaccinated against COVID-19. The COVID-19 **pandemic** shut down schools and businesses. Rodrigo stood at a podium and talked about the importance of vaccines and how they prevent serious illnesses. In 2024, Rodrigo encouraged young people to vote during the US presidential elections as well.

During the *GUTS* World Tour, Rodrigo launched Fund 4 Good. The fund supported organizations that worked to make a better future for girls and women. A portion of each ticket sale went to Fund 4 Good. At each tour stop, she helped a different organization. For the Canadian leg of her tour, Rodrigo donated funds to women's shelters. These shelters house women who are dealing with violence.

In 2021, Rodrigo met Vice President Kamala Harris at the White House.

In May 2024, the American Society of Composers, Authors, and Publishers named Rodrigo and Nigro songwriters of the year. Rodrigo had also claimed the award in 2022. Rodrigo spoke about how songwriting was an important part of her life. She enjoyed sharing her stories.

Rodrigo performed at a benefit concert to help raise money for communities affected by the Los Angeles, California, wildfires in January 2025.

By October 2024, Rodrigo had performed 95 sold-out shows on the *GUTS* World Tour. She also added more dates for her fans across the world. The tour had already made more than $186 million. She also released her concert film on Netflix titled *Olivia Rodrigo: GUTS World Tour*. The megastar was thrilled to share her performance with even more fans.

As a rising artist, Rodrigo has grown into a superstar. She took on acting roles at a young age even after being told no. Now she continues to use her songwriting and singing skills to express herself. Rodrigo also continues to earn awards for her music. She has used her voice to stand up for what she believes in, too. Fans are excited to see what the popular performer does next.

IN HER WORDS

Rodrigo spoke about being a role model to many young girls. She said:

> **"I've grown up with so many incredibly strong, talented, inspiring role models—women songwriters that I've looked up to for a long time. And when I look back, I think that all of them were my heroes particularly because they were exactly who they were, and they didn't censor parts of themselves or cherry-pick parts of themselves to present to the public."**

Source: Chang, Ailsa, and Kira Wakeam. "Olivia Rodrigo Wants You to Decide What Her Songs Are About." NPR, *September 26, 2023. www.npr.org.*

GLOSSARY

acclaimed (uh-KLAYMD) When something is acclaimed, it means that it is celebrated. Rodrigo's music is acclaimed.

auditioned (ah-DIH-shund) Auditioned means someone tried out for a role or performance. Rodrigo auditioned for the TV show *Bizaardvark*.

ballads (BA-ludz) Ballads are moving songs that usually have a slow tempo. Rodrigo played piano ballads at the *GUTS* World Tour.

censor (SEN-sur) To censor is to remove or get rid of something due to social expectations. Rodrigo looked up to women songwriters who did not censor parts of themselves.

debut (day-BYOO) A debut is the first time someone performs or shows something to the public. Rodrigo's debut album won Best Pop Vocal Album at the Grammy Awards.

deluxe (duh-LUKS) Something deluxe is regarded as special or costly. Rodrigo released the deluxe version of her second album titled *GUTS: spilled*.

demonstrated (DEH-mun-stray-tud) Something is demonstrated when it is shown clearly. Rodrigo demonstrated her songwriting skills on her song "drivers license."

heritage (HAYR-ih-tej) Heritage is something that is carried down from birth. Rodrigo has Filipino, Irish, and German heritage.

pandemic (pan-DEH-muk) A pandemic is an outbreak of a disease that spreads across many places. The COVID-19 pandemic shut down schools and businesses.

producers (pruh-DOO-sirs) Producers are people who supervise or pay for artistic projects. Rodrigo was asked to write a song for *HSM:TM:TS* by the show's music producers.

therapist (THAYR-uh-puhst) A therapist is a health care worker trained in specific methods of treatment for people with injuries or diseases. Rodrigo's father was a therapist.

FAST FACTS

★ Olivia Isabel Rodrigo was born on February 20, 2003, in Murrieta, California.

★ Olivia took singing, acting, and piano lessons at a young age. She also performed at talent shows and contests.

★ Olivia starred in *Grace Stirs Up Success*. She later landed leading roles on Disney shows such as *Bizaardvark* and *High School Musical: The Musical: The Series* (*HSM:TM:TS*).

★ Olivia released her first single, titled "drivers license," in January 2021. It was a huge hit. On May 21, she released her debut album, *SOUR*.

★ In September 2023, Rodrigo released her second album, titled *GUTS*. She toured the world performing popular songs off the album. She also started Fund 4 Good. Fund 4 Good helped organizations support the future of girls and women.

ONE STRIDE FURTHER

★ If you were going to write a song about your life, what would you write about? What tools or resources can help you write this song?

★ Rodrigo often expresses herself through music and songwriting. How do you like to express yourself? Why?

★ Rodrigo stands up for causes she cares about. What causes do you care about? How can you stand up for these causes?

★ At first, Rodrigo hated playing the piano, but she grew to love it. She uses the piano to help write songs. What do you think would have happened if she quit playing the piano? How do you know when to quit something or to keep trying?

FIND OUT MORE

IN THE LIBRARY

Gottlieb, Beth. *Olivia Rodrigo*. Buffalo, NY: Enslow Publishing, 2024.

Rose, Lisa. *Taylor Swift*. Parker, CO: The Child's Word, 2026.

Rose, Rachel. *Olivia Rodrigo: Actor and Singer*. Minneapolis, MN: Bearport Publishing Company, 2023.

ON THE WEB

Visit our website for links about Olivia Rodrigo:

childsworld.com/links

Note to Parents, Caregivers, Teachers, and Librarians: We routinely verify our web links to make sure they are safe and active sites. So encourage your readers to check them out!

INDEX